How To
Anger & Bitterness

Dr. Glen Spencer Jr.

Dr. Glen Spencer Jr.
15 Pine Ridge Rd — Tunkhannock, Pa. 18657
PastorGlenSpencer@gmail.com

Contents

It's A Mad World Out There!

Ecclesiastes 7:9

Be not hasty in thy spirit to be angry: for anger resteth in the bosom of fools. (Ecclesiastes 7:9) Anger has always been a problem. Way back in the beginning the Bible tells us that Cain was **very wroth. (Genesis 4:5)** As a result of Anger Cain went on to murder his brother Abel. Many sins are committed in anger. Nothing good come from this kind of anger.

**For the wrath of man worketh not the
righteousness of God. (James 1:20)**

Cain's anger brought him to faced the judgment of God for murdering his brother. The same is true today. Live are utterly ruined because of uncontrolled anger. There is no doubt that anger is a growing problem in our world today. A recent U.S. News poll showed that:

*"... a vast majority of Americans feel
their country has reached an ill-mannered*

5

watershed. Nine out of ten Americans think incivility is a serious problem, and nearly half think it is extremely serious. Seventy-eight percent say the problem has worsened in the last 10 years."

The world today is infested with angry and bitter people. They are slaves to these awful sins. Their whole life is discolored and defeated because they see every thing through the lens of anger. We see these sad circumstance everywhere.

- Angry kids going to school and shooting fellow students and or teachers.

- In U.S. workplaces, over 2 million people each year are victims of crimes—75 percent of which are assaults.

- The National Highway Traffic Safety Administration reported that *"Road rage is our #1 traffic problem."* A recent Gallup poll reported that motorists were more worried about road rage (42%) than about drunk driving (35%). (The New York Times).

- Aggressive driving has replaced drunken driving as the most-feared highway threat in the Washington, D.C., metropolitan area, and is a rising concern nationwide. Nationally, deaths and injuries attributed to aggressive driving have climbed 51 percent since 1990. (The American Automobile Association Foundation for Traffic Safety).

- Now we have *"Sideline rage."* Angry parents behaving so bad at youth sports events that 76% of respondents from 60 high school athletic associations said increased spectator interference is causing many officials to quit (Associated Press).

- Sports stars publicly display anger and violence on and off the court. They beat and spit on each other and even attack the officials. Attacks at sporting events for children are so prevalent, that the National Association of Sports Officials now offers assault insurance to members.

- Air Rage is a term used to describe irritated passengers who take their frustrations out on airline personnel.

It is evident that anger is a problem in our society. Both Christians and non-Christians battle with this sin. Webster defines the word **anger** as:

> *"A violent passion of the mind excited by a real or supposed injury; usually*

accompanied with a propensity to take vengeance, or to obtain satisfaction from the offending party."

The *"Baker Encyclopedia Of Psychology"* defines anger as *"an emotional readiness to aggress."* Such people are called *"Hot Heads."* Solomon said:

A fool's wrath is presently known...
(Proverbs 12:16)

Anger drives individuals to do things that tend to hurt or destroy. There are four words in the Bible that describe different types of anger.

The Exercise Of Indignation

Indignation describes anger that is the result of an injustice or sin committed against someone. Noah Webster defines indignation as:

"Anger or extreme anger, mingled with contempt, disgust or abhorrence ... The anger of a superior; extreme anger; particularly, the wrath of God against sinful men..."

Indignation is a righteous anger that is free from rage and retaliation. This type of anger alone isn't necessarily a sin; even God gets angry.

> ... God is angry with the wicked every day. (Psalm 7:11)

God's anger is righteous indignation. God's anger is never sinful. Jesus displayed this kind of anger. As we see in Scripture His anger was always a righteous and just.

> And he entered again into the synagogue; and there was a man there which had a withered hand. And they watched him, whether he would heal him on the sabbath day; that they might accuse him. And he saith unto the man which had the withered hand, Stand forth. And he saith unto them, Is it lawful to do good on the sabbath days, or to do evil? to save life, or to kill? But they held their peace. And when he had looked round about on them with anger, being grieved for the hardness of their hearts, he saith unto the man, Stretch forth thine hand. And he stretched it out: and his hand was restored whole as the other. And the Pharisees went forth, and straightway took counsel with the Herodians against him, how they might destroy him. (Mark 3:1-6)

The Pharisees were more concerned with their observance of the sabbath than they were with the needs of this man. They were dedicated to their dead, legalistic religion while ignoring the needs of the hurting. This injustice angered the Lord. However, notice that although Jesus was angry ...

✦ He didn't explode into a fit of rage.

✦ He didn't seek vengeance and destroy them.

✦ He didn't hold on to it allowing it to fester and turn to bitterness.

✦ He didn't suppress His anger.

Instead Jesus reached out to the victim rather than retaliating against the offenders. He didn't respond in a way that would be sinful or ruin His testimony or stir up more strife.

The Explosion Of Rage

Rage is a short fused and uncontrolled anger. It is a dangerous and destructive *"blow your top," "fly off the handle"* kind of anger. It is the kind of anger Solomon was speaking of when he said:

> **A fool's wrath is presently known...**
> **(Proverbs 12:16)**

This is a deadly and disastrous kind of anger. It's the kind of anger that made Cain kill Abel. It's the kind of anger that cost Saul his throne. It's the kind of anger made Moses smite the rock twice. Rage is a destructive and sinful kind of anger. This is the kind of anger that is wrecking our society today. Someone described rage as:

> "... a fervent exasperation full of energy and characterized by forcefulness of expression and intensity of emotion."

Many sins are committed in the wake of this kind of anger. Nothing good comes from rage.

For the wrath of man worketh not the righteousness of God. (James 1:20)

Rage is uncontrolled anger that is destructive and sinful and violates the principle of self-control as taught in the Scriptures. Such people are walking time bombs with hair trigger tempers ready to blow up at any second.

The Enlargement Of Wrath

Wrath is a *"violent anger."* Unlike rage which is quick and over within a few minutes, wrath is an anger that desires and peruses revenge. It is an anger that is never satisfied or settled. It is an ever increasing kind of anger. The word **wrath** carries the idea of *"swelling with anger."* It is a boiling resentment. Earl White said:

> *"It derives from a desire of the flesh to strike out at anything that threatens self interests. It is a desire to take vengeance out of the hands of God and take it to ourselves."*

Wrath is an anger that holds grudges. It is a get even, retaliatory anger. The wrathful person is not satisfied until they see their offender hurt. It is an **eye for an eye, and a tooth for a tooth** philosophy that demands justice. This is a no grace, no forgiveness, get even kind of anger. With this kind of anger there is no compassion and no control. It will reach the point where strikes out. It is the kind of anger that caused Cain to murder Abel.

> **And Cain talked with Abel his brother: and it came to pass, when they were in the field, that Cain rose up against Abel his brother, and slew him. (Genesis 4:8)**

Many people, even many Christian's are eaten up with this kind of anger. It is an anger that results from a failure to forgive. It is a sin against God and the brethren.

And be ye kind one to another, tenderhearted, forgiving one another, even as God for Christ's sake hath forgiven you. (Ephesians 4:32)

The failure to forgive will ruin our life. Of all of the people in the world, Christians should understand and exercise forgiveness the most. We have experienced the greatest kind of forgiveness. God help us to show the same forgiveness to others.

The Enmity Of Resentment

Resentment is a stubborn, long burning, long lasting kind of anger. This an anger that is held on to and rests in the heart.

Be not hasty in thy spirit to be angry, for anger resteth in the bosom of fools. (Ecclesiastes 7:9b)

The word **resteth** means that the anger abides there. Like all anger, resentment can be the result of a real or an imaginary offense. Resentment is a self-pitying, suppressed anger that stews and seethes deep down inside a person and eventually turns into bitterness that sours the whole life. Someone said, *"resentment is like taking poison and waiting for the other person to die."* This is where bitterness gets a hold in one's life.

Resentment was the kind of anger that ruined the elder brother of the prodigal. He had been a faithful son and stayed the course and he was quick to point that out to his father. The prodigal was an unfaithful son who had taken his inheritance and squandered it away on fast and free living. Upon coming back home the father threw a party and celebrated his return. Rather than rejoicing, the elder brother was overcome with anger. The Bible says:

And he was angry... (Luke 15:28)

The elder brother had stayed when his brother strayed. That is commendable. However, his problem was that he was angered by his brother's departure and he let his anger lead him into bitterness. Now he resented his brother. He resented the father's celebration and the receiving of his wayward brother back into the family. Resentment is an anger that takes over your life. Resentful people allow their anger to burn and fester until it permeates their whole life.

The Outward Signs Of Anger

Proverbs 23:7

For as he thinketh in his heart, so is he... **(Proverbs 23:7)** Anger has a demeanor about it and is most of the time easily recognized. When someone is bitter, we don't have to guess at it—their behavior will show it. Anger often shows up on the face.

> **But unto Cain and to his offering he had not respect. And Cain was very wroth, and his countenance fell. (Genesis 4:5)**

But not only can you see anger on the face, it also shows up in actions.

> **And Cain talked with Abel his brother: and it came to pass, when they were in the field, that Cain rose up against Abel his brother, and slew him. (Genesis 4:8)**

The murder of Abel started with the anger of Cain. Cain's problem was a heart problem. If he had properly dealt with his anger, there wouldn't have been a murder that day. Jesus said:

All these evil things come from within, and defile the man. (Mark 7:23)

Jesus was teaching us a very basic principle here. The heart directs the life. We live from the inside out. Solomon taught the same truth. Speaking of man's heart said:

... out of it are the issues of life. (Proverbs 4:23)

The heart is the home of the personal life. A man's life follows his heart.

For as he thinketh in his heart, so is he... (Proverbs 23:7)

Though it is an exercise in futility, folks often try to hide what they are, but sooner or later their life reveals the truth. Anger that is allowed to linger in your heart will eventually lunge into your life. There is no such thing as successfully hiding anger. Lets look at some of the signs of anger.

The Problem Of Pride

Pride is the grandfather of all sin. Anger and bitterness flourish in the heart of a prideful person. Prideful and jealous Simon serves as an example. Paul identified Simon's problem as bitterness.

> For I perceive that thou art in the gall
> of bitterness, and in the bond of iniquity.
> (Acts 8:23)

The **gall of bitterness** speaks of excessive bitterness that comes from the **bond of iniquity.** Bitter people are slaves to sin. One of the dreadful effects of sin is bitterness. We can see from the context what actually motivated Simon and caused his bitterness.

The Pride

But there was a certain man, called Simon, which beforetime in the same city used sorcery, and bewitched the people of Samaria, giving out that himself was some great one. (Acts 8:9) Simon went around **giving out that himself was some great one.** Pride is a breeding ground for anger and bitterness! Angry people are always jockeying for position and pomp. This is one of the reasons that angry people don't do well with authority. They want to be the authority. They want to be recognized and applauded. They attempt to rise to the top by lifting themselves up. They may try to hide it with a false humility, but it will be apparent. Like Simon, an angry man usually goes around trying **... giving out that himself was some great one. (Acts 8:9)**

This is the kind of pride that ruins men and alienates them from God. They might put on as if they are some great one, but in reality they are far from God. A man who truly love the Lord will hate pride.

> **The fear of the LORD is to hate evil: pride, and arrogancy, and the evil way, and the froward mouth, do I hate. (Proverbs 8:13)**

What an ugly sin pride is. The word **arrogancy** carries the idea of *"swelling"* and pictures someone who thinks of and presents himself as bigger and greater than he really is. Pride is what we perceive our self to be. Humility is coming to grips with who we really are. Because pride offends God we are to hate it. Why? Because God hates it.

> **These six things doth the LORD hate: yea, seven are an abomination unto him: A proud look … (Proverbs 6:16-17)**

Notice that God begins the list with pride. Pride is a big problem in the world today. And it is probably one of the biggest problem we have in Christianity. Remember that pride was born in the heart of Satan (Isaiah 14:12-18). Pride ruined him and it will ruin us. We stand in awe at the audacity of Satan for attempting to rule on God's throne. Yet, we do the same thing when we refuse God His sovereign right to rule our life. Pride was the sin that destroyed God's creation and it remains the sin that is destroying men's lives. Pride is the sin that turned Lucifer into the Devil.

The Pretense

To whom they all gave heed, from the least to the greatest, saying, This man is the great power of God. (Acts 8:10) Wicked Simon had a standing that angry and bitter people love. He had a testimony among the people as having **the great power of God.** The self-made **great one** was in the spotlight. He had a place of prominence. Although, the people believed that Simon was a man with great supernatural power, he was nevertheless an unsaved and ungodly man. Bitter people can put on a pretty good show, but inside they are far from what they seem.

The Perversion

And to him they had regard, because that of long time he had bewitched them with sorceries. (Acts 8:10-11) We have already learned that Simon was a fake! The people thought he was wonderful, but he was as wicked as the Devil in his heart. Unsuspecting people didn't know that he had **bewitched** them. The word **bewitched** means *"fascinated"* or *"charmed."* An angry person knows how to get a following. He charms people with flattery, favor and gifts in order to gain their confidence and control them. They work and manipulate people in order to get what they want. We will look at this in more detail later on.

The Petition

And when Simon saw that through laying on of the apostles' hands the Holy Ghost was given, he offered them money, Saying, Give me also this power, that on whomsoever I lay hands, he may receive the Holy Ghost. (Acts 8:18-19) What Simon really is in his heart now begins to show in his life. He was so hungry for attention and power that he offered to buy the Holy Ghost with money! An angry and bitter person is never satisfied with the place God gives him. They starve for more attention, more position, more power and so on. God did not exalt Simon therefore, he set out to gain glory on his own. The Bible tells us how to be exalted.

> **Humble yourselves therefore under the mighty hand of God, that he may exalt you in due time. (1 Peter 5:6)**

Simon was eaten up with **the gall of bitterness, and in the bond of iniquity. (Acts 8:23)** A bitter person is never satisfied. If someone else has a place of prestige or power, an angry person will never be satisfied until he moves in on it. He is constantly competing, cheating and clamoring to gain the applause of men.

The Problem

Thou hast neither part nor lot in this matter: for thy heart is not right in the sight of God. (Acts 8:21) An angry and bitter person's heart is out of tune with God. Simon's heart was to lift himself up instead of Christ. Simon wanted to be number one. Simon was a status seeker. But as a result of his pride and desire to be on top and be recognized as number one—he ended up bitter. Bitter people are often glory-mongers who maneuver and manipulate their way through life. They are consumed with a need to be recognized for their self-conceived greatness. John the Baptist serves as an example of a powerful man who had a true heart concerning this matter. Speaking of Jesus, John said, **He must increase, but I must decrease. (John 3:30)**

The Maneuvering Of Manipulation

An angry person is usually very shrewd and cunning. He will be crafty and clever in maneuvering and manipulating people in order to get what he wants or what he thinks he deserves. Absalom is a good example of this kind of anger. Most are familiar with the Biblical account of Amnon raping his half-sister Tamar. The Bible says when Absalom heard about it that he:

> **... spake unto his brother Amnon neither good nor bad: for Absalom hated Amnon, because he had forced his sister Tamar. (2 Samuel 13:22)**

Absalom's anger burned in his heart for **two full years. (2 Samuel 13:23)** As a result, Absalom schemed up a plan to kill Amnon. He instructed his servant to wait till Amnon was drunk and kill him. They carried out Absalom's orders and Amnon was dead (2 Samuel 13:29). After Absalom killed his brother, he spent several years in exile with his mother's people in Geshur. Afterwards, David allowed Absalom to return home, but refused to see him for two full years.

> **And the king said, Let him turn to his own house, and let him not see my face. So Absalom returned to his own house, and saw not the king's face ... So Absalom dwelt two full years in Jerusalem, and saw not the king's face. (2 Samuel 14:24, 28)**

By now Absalom's anger and bitterness was also burning and festering against his father David. Absalom wasn't just angry over Tamar's rape. That is where it started, but he was angry about the whole course of events, including David's failure to discipline and deal with Amnon for his crime. Absalom had taken matters into his own hand and David was shunning him. Now Absalom is seeking vengeance on his father by plotting ways to overthrow him and gain power for himself. Absalom schemed and manipulated until he eventually :

... stole the hearts of the men of Israel. (2 Samuel 15:6)

What stands out here is the dishonest scheming and manipulation that Absalom used to steal the hearts of David's people. Notice the flattery.

And Absalom said unto him, See, thy matters are good and right. (2 Samuel 15:3)

Absalom says, *"you sure do have a case." "You are in the right."* Remember, the word flattery means to *"speak smoothly."* Absalom was telling them what they wanted to hear. He is speaking smooth words in order to get an advantage over the King.

> **A man that flattereth his neighbour spreadeth a net for his feet. (Proverbs 29:5)**

The flattery continues:

> **And it was so, that when any man came nigh to him to do him obeisance, he put forth his hand, and took him, and kissed him. (2 Samuel 15:5)**

Look at the political maneuvering and manipulation! When someone approached Absalom with a show of reverence, he would extend his hand, as one would with an equal. Now he is campaigning. He is looking for votes as it were. Shaking hands, hugging, and kissing on people that he normally wouldn't spend a minute with, all because he needs them. An angry person knows how to flatter and work people.

Next, we see him working against the authority of the King. He cleverly says:

> **... but there is no man deputed of the king to hear thee. (2 Samuel 15:3)**

This is sedition! He is looking to steal the loyalty of the people away from God's ordained authority in their life. We see this happen in a lot in our day. The wrong kind of friend can steal the parents authority and take over a young person's life. A leader or someone else in the Church can steal the Pastor's authority away from him. These things happen all of the time. Notice that Absalom pointed out how the King had apparently failed the people in this area. Look at his slyness, his cunning—he is downright deceitful. Notice how he is careful not to come right out against the King, but he does make the King look bad. Here comes the manipulation.

Absalom said moreover, Oh that I were made judge in the land, that every man which hath any suit or cause might come unto me, and I would do him justice!. (2 Samuel 15:4) Like a wolf with no character he is undermining the King by manipulating the people. He is taking a need of the people and using it to shed a bad light on David and a good light on himself. He is selling himself to the people as the answer to their problems. All of Absalom's smooth talk is nothing but a maneuver to lure the people into his net. He is gaining control of them. This is what Les Carter and Frank Minirth call the *"passive-aggressive anger sneak."*

> *"Passive aggression is caused by a need to have control with the least amount of vulnerability. This form of anger is different from suppression in that the person knows he or she is angry (in*

contrast to suppressed anger, which is denied) But because this person assumes it is too risky to be open, he or she frustrates others by subtle sabotage. The need for control is evidence of a strong competitive spirit. Whereas healthy relationships do not keep score regarding right and wrong, the passive aggressive person is out to win. Like the openly aggressive person, the passive aggressive person is engaged in a battle for superiority ... sly forms of handling anger tend to keep him or her in the driver's seat."

Notice their definition and how it fits Absalom's anger. Absalom was scheming to get into the driver's seat. Angry people want power and they will do anything to get it. Angry people are always competing for positions of authority or any place for that matter where they can be lifted up. This kind of anger and bitterness stems from pride, jealously and envy.

The Iniquity Of Intimidation

Intimidation is another favorite tool of an angry person. Instead of being Spirit led, they are flesh driven. They are bullies whose only concern is getting ahead no matter who they have to destroy in the process. David's brother Eliab is a good example of an angry man who resorted to intimidation to achieve his ends. Eliab was a man who needed attention. Like Simon and Absalom, he was a glory monger. He was no doubt a great man so far as his stature was concerned. When the people considered Eliab's form and physique, they said:

> **Surely the LORD'S anointed is before him. (1 Samuel 16:6)**

However, God said:

> **... Look not on his countenance, or on the height of his stature; because I have refused him: for the LORD seeth not as man seeth; for man looketh on the outward appearance, but the LORD looketh on the heart. (1 Samuel 16:7)**

God doesn't look for what a man is on the outside. So far as his outward form Eliab was the greatest, but his heart wasn't right. God knew something about Eliab that the people didn't know. Eliab was more concerned about his outer appearance, than he was the inner condition of his heart.

> **And Eliab his eldest brother heard when he spake unto the men; and Eliab's anger was kindled against David, and he said, Why camest thou down hither? and**

with whom hast thou left those few sheep in the wilderness? I know thy pride, and the naughtiness of thine heart; for thou art come down that thou mightest see the battle. (1 Samuel 17:28)

When David's zeal and concern for God shed a bad light on Eliab and the other cowards of Saul's army. **Eliab's anger was kindled** and he responded with intimidation. His first slam was **Why camest thou down hither?** The insinuation was that David had no business being there. Notice that David's being there was no problem until he pointed out that something needed to be done about Goliath. Suddenly Eliab became angry and his response was basically, *"Who do you think you are! What is a ruddy little punk like you even doing around us great soldiers."* Eliab's second slam was, **with whom hast thou left those few sheep in the wilderness.** The shepherd's job was a lowly one. Certainly nothing near as glorious as that of a great warrior. Eliab pointed out that David's work was not only the lowly work of tending sheep, but just a **few** sheep. Eliab was trying to bully and intimidate David. This is a tactic of a bitter person.

The Pretense Of Pouting

An angry person loves attention. Therefore, anger often manifests itself in pouting and sulking. It is very common for someone who is angry and bitter to get caught up in the martyr's syndrome and go into a "woe is me" routine when they do not get their way. Pouting and sulking is another of their control and manipulation techniques. Let's look at a couple of examples from the Bible.

The Pouting King

Ahab is a good example of this kind of pouting and sulking behavior. Nothing is more pitiful that a grown man or woman acting like a spoiled child. In 1 Kings 21 when Ahab wanted Naboth's vineyard and Naboth refused to sell it to him the Bible says:

> **And Ahab came into his house heavy and displeased because of the word which Naboth the Jezreelite had spoken to him: for he had said, I will not give thee the inheritance of my fathers. And he laid him down upon his bed, and turned away his face, and would eat no bread. (1 Kings 21:4)**

Now look at the mighty King Ahab! He is throwing himself quite the pity party! Wicked Jezebel comes and finds him sulking in the bed like a baby and refusing to cat.

But Jezebel his wife came to him, and said unto him, Why is thy spirit so sad, that thou eatest no bread?. (1 Kings 21:5)

Here is a man that is supposed to be the leader of a nation. His foolish wife comes and plays right into his hand. An angry person will find someone to support him in his endeavors. The sad thing is that he usually ends up taking his supporter down with him. There are whole families eaten up with anger and bitterness because the husband or the wife has infected the whole household. Ahab proceeds to tell Jezebel how that mean old Naboth wouldn't give him his way. His pity party pulled at the heart string of Jezebel. She then set out to see to it that Naboth was killed so that old pouting Ahab could have his vineyard. Ahab had used his pouting and sulking to manipulate Jezebel into taking action on his behalf. Wickedness knows no boundaries.

The Pouting Prophet

Jonah is another example of an angry man pouting because he didn't get his way. God had sent a mighty revival to Nineveh. The whole city was saved and spared. You would think that such a work of God would please anyone, especially a preacher. But look how Jonah reacted.

But it displeased Jonah exceedingly, and he was very angry. (Jonah 4:1)

Here we see Jonah mad and greatly displeased with God. An angry man is hard to please. He has his mind set on what he wants and nothing else will do. This is the account of anger and bitterness completely discoloring a man's perspective, even to the point that he is angry with for showing mercy to others. Jonah flat out tells God why he is mad.

> **And he prayed unto the LORD, and said, I pray thee, O LORD, was not this my saying, when I was yet in my country? Therefore I fled before unto Tarshish: for I knew that thou art a gracious God, and merciful, slow to anger, and of great kindness, and repentest thee of the evil. (Jonah 4:2)**

Think about this! Jonah did not want Nineveh spared! God spared Nineveh in spite of Jonah's wishes. Now look at Jonah.

> **Therefore now, O LORD, take, I beseech thee, my life from me; for it is better for me to die than to live. (Jonah 4:3)**

Well here is the pity party! Oh God since I didn't get my way I wish I could just die! Now, this is a preacher acting like this and look what he did next.

So Jonah went out of the city, and sat on the east side of the city, and there made him a booth, and sat under it in the shadow, till he might see what would become of the city. (Jonah 4:5)

Jonah thought that if he pouted long enough that God would eventually destroy the city. Eaten up with anger and bitterness Jonah sat and watched the city just waiting for its destruction. He wanted the Judgment of God to come upon them. An angry man is a very self-centered man. He is not concerned about others—only himself. So God prepared a gourd to teach Jonah an important lesson.

And the LORD God prepared a gourd, and made it to come up over Jonah, that it might be a shadow over his head, to deliver him from his grief. So Jonah was exceeding glad of the gourd. But God prepared a worm when the morning rose the next day, and it smote the gourd that it withered. (Jonah 4:6-7)

Now notice Jonah's response.

> And it came to pass, when the sun did arise, that God prepared a vehement east wind; and the sun beat upon the head of Jonah, that he fainted, and wished in himself to die, and said, It is better for me to die than to live. (Jonah 4:8)

The mercy and grace of God in sparing the people of Nineveh meant nothing to poor pouting Jonah. He cared more for the gourd than he did for the whole city of Nineveh. Jonah **wished in himself to die, and said, It is better for me to die than to live.** How self-centered and selfish can you get. Jonah could not see beyond his own selfish demands.

> And God said to Jonah, Doest thou well to be angry for the gourd? And he said, I do well to be angry, even unto death. Then said the LORD, Thou hast had pity on the gourd, for the which thou hast not laboured, neither madest it grow; which came up in a night, and perished in a night: And should not I spare Nineveh, that great city, wherein are more than sixscore thousand persons that cannot discern between their right hand and their left hand; and also much cattle?. (Jonah 4:9-11)

God pleaded with Jonah to be reasonable reminds him that there were **more than sixscore thousand persons that cannot discern between their right hand and their left hand.** Think about that! Over 120,000 babies and young children in Nineveh. With that many children in the city of Nineveh there were probably a total population of six hundred thousand to a million people. Jonah's anger against the people of Nineveh had so hardened his heart that he would rather have seen the whole city go to Hell, just to have his own way. This book ends with Jonah in pity party, eaten up with bitterness, mad at God and everyone else. What a tragic end to a man's life.

"*Of the seven deadly sins, anger is possibly the most fun. To lick your wounds, to smack your lips over grievances long past, to savor to the last toothsome morsel both the pain you are given and the pain you are giving back. In many ways it is a feast fit for a king. The chief drawback is that what you are wolfing down is yourself. The skeleton at the feast is you.*"

—*Frederick Buechner*

When Anger Turns To Bitterness

Luke 15

There are several Bible examples of anger festering and growing into bitterness. We could name Naomi, Saul, Absalom, Ahithophel, Jonah, and others. However, we will look at the prodigal's elder brother who serves as a New Testament example of how anger can fester and develop until it springs up in bitterness. When anger develops into bitterness it takes over and ruins one's life.

Bitterness is a deep seated heart that has been soured by harboring animosity, envy, resentment, revenge, unforgiveness, and grudges for another's offenses. Paul describes bitterness as the state of those who have failed of the grace of God and therefore, troubled and defiled.

> **Looking diligently lest any man fail of the grace of God; lest any root of bitterness springing up trouble you, and thereby many be defiled. (Hebrews 12:15)**

When we fail to draw upon God's grace to sweeten our life—bitterness will take over. Remember, bitterness is always self-inflicted. Bitterness is not something that someone can do to us. We cause our own bitterness. Bitterness is anger in its most poisonous stage. It is a deep seated anger that has stewed deep down inside until it's poison rules the heart. It is the most dangerous form of anger. Bitterness destroys people, marriages, families, relationships, and Churches. Bitterness will completely destroy you. Bitterness is holding onto an offense until it has a hold on you. Someone has said:

> *Bitterness is anger that is so deep and so pervasive that it colors a person's entire perception of life.*

Bitterness will rip the joy of God from our heart. In our Lord's parable of the prodigal, the elder son is an example of that kind of bitterness. He completely missed the Father's joy and the repentance of his lost brother. He was so focused on the offense that bitterness engulfed his soul.

The Curse Of Bitterness

Anger and bitterness cannot be hidden. It always manifests itself. When anger is not dealt with it takes root in the heart continuing to infect until it becomes full blown bitterness. Like a cancer that initially starts in one place, but spreads throughout the body, anger and bitterness start in the heart and eventually takes over the whole life. Such is the case with the elder brother. He had held on to his brother's offense until it had a hold on him.

The Resentful Indifference

When he heard of his brother's return **he was angry, and would not go in. (Luke 15:28a)** When you think about it, this is a sad state of affairs. Here is a man who couldn't be happy though God had wrought a great miracle. God had brought his brother home yet, his response was anger. He rejoiced not! He wouldn't even go into the house where his family and friends had gathered with his brother.

The Rejoicing Interrupted

Take note of how the Father responded to the elder son. The Bible says **therefore came his father out, and entreated him. (Luke 15:28b)** The Father had to leave the rejoicing and the celebration to go out and deal with the angry and bitter son. Oh! How bitterness must grieve the heart of God. In Ephesians chapter 4, Paul listed several sins that needed to be put off. In his list he mentioned anger in one form or another five times, **angry. (26)**; **wrath (26)**;

bitterness (31); **wrath (31)**; and **anger (31)** In the context of that passage Paul warned **And grieve not the holy Spirit of God, whereby ye are sealed unto the day of redemption. (Ephesians 4:30)** The sins of anger and bitterness grieve the Holy Spirit. When we are bitter we are out of touch with God's grace.

What makes God happy is the sinner's return. **I say unto you, that likewise joy shall be in heaven over one sinner that repenteth... (Luke 15:7)** Bitterness will cause you to focus on the offense, but God's heart is to forgive and restore. Grace does not keep records, but anger does. Bitterness will bring rejoicing to a halt. Bitterness is the reason for so many Churches and homes being miserable and unhappy places. Just like the angry and bitter son ruined the Father's rejoicing, many today have sucked the joy out of other people's lives. Furthermore, they have grieved the heart of God. Bitter people ruin the happiness and rejoicing of others.

The Resulting Insolence

And he answering said to his father, Lo, these many years do I serve thee, neither transgressed I at any time thy commandment: and yet thou never gavest me a kid, that I might make merry with my friends: But as soon as this thy son was come, which hath devoured thy living with harlots, thou

hast killed for him the fatted calf. (Luke 15:29-30) Look at this son's disrespectful attitude toward his father. Notice how he addresses the father. He starts off by saying **Lo.** Webster defines the **"Lo"** as a word *"used to excite particular attention in a hearer to some object of sight, or subject of discourse."* It is a statement that demands attention. He is basically saying to his father, "You be quiet an listen to me." "I have something to say to you." They may try to put across the illusion that they are submissive and faithful, but in their heart they are disobedient and hard. The elder had stayed by the stuff. He had worked hard and served his father. But as soon as the father displeased him he became angry and lashed out at him.

Look at what he said next. **But as soon as this thy son was come…** You can almost hear the scorn in his voice. An angry person will have a disrespectful heart and a critical attitude—especially toward those in authority. Notice that he didn't say, *"my brother,"* but **thy son.** Not only was he angry and bitter at his brother, but now he was angry at his father for showing mercy the his wayward son.

The Cause Of Bitterness

The prodigal was an unfaithful son who had taken his inheritance and squandered it away on fast and free living. Upon coming back home the father threw a party and celebrated his return. The elder brother, who had stayed the course and done the work in his brother's absence was overcome with anger. The Bible says, **And he was angry…. (Luke 15:28)** He resented his brother. He resented the father's celebration and the receiving his wayward brother back into the family.

The Offense That Disturbed Him

Notice where the elder son was. He was **in the field. (Luke 15:25)** He was on the job! He had been a faithful son. He stayed the course and he was quick to point that out to his father. But while he worked he couldn't get his mind off of the younger brother's offense.

> **But as soon as this thy son was come, which hath devoured thy living with harlots, thou hast killed for him the fatted calf. (Luke 15:30)**

The elder's bitterness boiled down to one offense. Remember, bitterness is holding onto an offense until it has a hold on you. His brother had left the farm. He ran off and wasted his inheritance on fast and free living while the older brother stayed on the farm and worked. Yes! The older brother stayed, but all the while, down in his heart he resented his brother's actions. The elder brother had never abandoned his father and run off to the far country, but he had the far country in his heart.

The Outlook That Damaged Him

And he answering said to his father, Lo, these many years do I serve thee, neither transgressed I at any time thy commandment: and yet thou never gavest me a kid, that I might make merry with my friends. (Luke 15:29) The elder got himself into a pity party mode. He focused on his brother's offense until it ate him up inside. His pride took over his life. Notice this! **I, I, ME, I,** and **MY.** Five personal pronouns in one verse. The elder brother had become self-centered, self-righteous, and selfish. An angry and bitter person will always rehearse and brag about their faithfulness. One reasons the older brother couldn't rejoice is because he was no longer the center of attention. Up until now he had the attention—he was the one who stayed. But now, the prodigal had the attention—he was the one who came back. Many times an angry person will be very competitive when it comes to recognition for their achievement—they don't like sharing the spotlight.

Don't assume that just because someone is knee deep in service that they are right with God. Activity is not necessarily a sign of affection. This boy served, but he didn't serve out of love for the father. His wasn't loving devotion it was lingering duty. Someone had to do it so he did. Now he was presenting himself as the martyr. **I, I, ME, I,** and **MY. (5:29)** He served because he was supposed to. It was simply a matter of duty for him. A lot of people get bitter because their service is not out of love for the Lord. They will serve for recognition, reward, promotion, or just because they are supposed to do it. My friend, when your service is not out of love for the Lord you will end up bitter in your life.

The elder son's pride caused him to focus on all that he had done for the father rather than what the Father had done for him. The saddest part of this whole account is the elder brother's attitude toward a repentant sinner. Though he had stayed and served the Father, he was completely out of touch with the Father's heart. The Bible says:

> **I say unto you, that likewise joy shall be in heaven over one sinner that repenteth, more than over ninety and nine just persons, which need no repentance. (Luke 15:7)**

The Father was delighted in the son that stayed on the job, but he was just a delighted over the one who came back. The elder brother was so steeped in bitterness that he could not enjoy the father's bestowal of grace upon his brother. He was caught up in the martyr's syndrome. He couldn't see past his own little world. He was out of touch with the Father's heart. The Father's heart is to see the sinner return. This is beautifully illustrated in this parable. The Bible says that the prodigal:

> **... arose, and came to his father. But when he was yet a great way off, his father saw him, and had compassion, and ran, and fell on his neck, and kissed him. (Luke 15:20)**

Notice how the father not only wanted the son's return he was looking for the son's return. **When he was yet a great way off, his father saw him.** The older brother wasn't looking, but the father was.

If we allow anger and bitterness in our heart it will take us out of touch with God's grace. Everything will become a system of do's and don'ts. A bitter person is one who keeps records of wrongs and knows nothing of grace. As a result he lives a sad and sour life.

The Oppression That Defeated Him

After rehearsing his faithfulness he said to his father, **thou never gavest me a kid, that I might** make merry with my friends. (Luke 15:29) Listen to him! **Thou never gavest me...** The whole thing seemed to boil down to a goat and a party. A goat took precedence over his brothers return. Jesus said, **And he was angry, and would not go in.... (Luke 15:28)** Bitterness will ruin your spiritual perspective. This elder son had accomplished a lot of good things. He had denied himself. He stayed on the job. He was faithful so far as his duties were concerned. But he failed so far as his devotion was concerned. Instead of focusing on his relationship with the father, he focused on his brothers failures and it soured his whole being. While the elder son I served, he allowed the root of bitterness to sprout and take hold of his heart. When the prodigal returned his bitterness sprang up and troubled him.

The Cure For Bitterness

The older brother had experienced the same grace that his brother did, but he couldn't see it. He was blinded by his self-righteousness. He had boasted:

> **Lo, these many years do I serve thee, neither transgressed I at any time thy commandment. (Luke 15:29)**

Actually, he was transgressing his Father's commandment at that very moment. His Father wanted him to go in and enjoy the celebration , but he was angry and refused. The older brother wasn't as high and mighty as he thought he was. Anger and bitterness causes us to think too highly of ourselves. It blinds us as too our own failures and faults. Note the two-fold cure to bitterness seen here.

The Abiding Presence Of The Father

The Father said, **Son, thou art ever with me. (Luke 15:31a)** The older brother allowed his bitterness to hinder his relationship with the Father. He missed what he needed most. He failed to realize the Father's presence. The Father had been there all along. They worked together. The ate together. They slept under the same roof. But they did not have a good relationship. Bitter people get out of touch with God. God has promised:

> **I will never leave thee, nor forsake thee. (Hebrews 13:5)**

No matter what others do to us lets remember that we a have a good and gracious God who delight to dwell with us.

The Abundant Possessions Of The Father

Next the Father said, **all that I have is thine. (Luke 15:31b)** The elder son had just accused the

Father of not giving him a goat so that he could have a party with his friends. Yet, the Fathers says, **all that I have is thine.** Anger and bitterness will blind you concerning the goodness and grace of God. He was fussing about a goat when he had the whole flock—he had the whole farm and everything that went with it. One of the ways to overcome bitterness is by realizing our blessings. Not matter what someone else may have done to us or taken from us, our great God has given us so much more than we deserve.

> **Let all bitterness, and wrath, and anger, and clamour, and evil speaking, be put away from you, with all malice: And be ye kind one to another, tenderhearted, forgiving one another, even as God for Christ's sake hath forgiven you. (Ephesians 4:31-32)**

Digging Out The Roots Of Bitterness

Hebrews 12:15

The Christian is to be sweet—not sour. However, many are harboring bitterness and unless it is dealt with, it will eventually permeate and sour the entire life. Bitterness is described as a **root ... springing up. (Hebrews 12:15)** It is s likened to a dangerous weed growing in a bed of flowers. At first it is just a root under the soil unseen. However, it is there stealing the nourishment, ruining the soil and starving the flowers, until at last it springs up choking and destroying the rest of the life in the garden. Failure to weed out the root of bitterness will ensure defeat in your life. Let's look at what the Bible says about *Digging Out The Roots Of Bitterness.*

Rely On The Grace Of God

Looking diligently lest any man fail of the grace of God; lest any root of bitterness springing up trouble you, and thereby many be defiled. (Hebrews 12:15) Bitterness is a dangerous and dreadful sin. Notice the command **Looking**

diligently. The utmost attention must be given to this matter of bitterness. We must look for it and find it before we can deal with it. If you have bitterness in your heart you will find it. The Bible says:

> **The heart knoweth his own bitterness. (Proverbs 14:10)**

Bitter people know that they are bitter whether they will admit it or not. Their own heart testifies to the fact that they are bitter. Not only are we to look diligently, but we can ask God to search us and find our bitterness.

> **Search me, O God, and know my heart: try me, and know my thoughts. (Psalm 139:23)**

We must apply ourselves to the task of finding and rooting out any bitterness. Paul goes on to explain, **lest any man fail of the grace of God.** If you are bitter you have failed of the grace of God. Isn't it interesting that God tied man's bitterness to failing of the grace of God? As the people of God we are dependent upon **the grace of God.** This truth is paramount in digging out the roots of bitterness. The Bible declares:

> **Where sin abounded, grace did much more abound. (Romans 5:20)**

The word **abound** carries the idea of *"super abounding"* and means *"to surpass by far, exceed immeasurably, or overflow beyond."* This is where we get victory! If we will live by the standard of grace we will never get bitter because grace will *surpass by far, exceed immeasurably,* and *overflow beyond* the offense that would normally anger us. No wonder God said:

> **My grace is sufficient for thee: for my strength is made perfect in weakness. (2 Corinthians 12:9)**

People who are bitter have failed to draw upon God's grace. We must draw constantly upon God's grace in order to be victorious in overcoming bitterness. We must reside in the throne room of God.

> **Let us therefore come boldly unto the throne of grace, that we may obtain mercy, and find grace to help in time of need. (Hebrews 4:16)**

This verse pictures the believer entering into to the throne room of God to find the grace we need to overcome our sin—including anger and bitterness.

Respond Correctly To Offenses

Jesus said, **It is impossible but that offences will come. (Luke 17:1)** You might as well go ahead and accept the fact that you are going to get your toes stepped on. You are going to get offended. There are going to be some things that rub you the wrong way. So how do we respond correctly? It is simple! We must ACT rather than REACT. We deal with a root of bitterness by acting biblically rather than reacting in the flesh. We don't have a choice in many of the things that happen to us, but we do have a choice over how we respond. We need to think biblically in order to act biblically. When bitterness is running one's life he does not think spiritually. Once the root of bitterness takes hold and springs up, it is manifest in selfishness, pride, a competitive spirit, a controlling and manipulative lifestyle, anger, evil speaking, clamor, rage, resentment, retaliation and so on. But if we are thinking biblically we will act differently. The Psalmist wrote:

Great peace have they which love thy law: and nothing shall offend them. (Psalm 119:165)

Here is the key to acting biblically. When I am in the word of God and I love the word of God like I am supposed to, your offenses toward me will not offend me. You can even try to offend me and it will not work because I am full of the word of God and the word governs my life. Paul said:

Let the word of Christ dwell in you richly in all wisdom; teaching and admonishing one another in psalms and hymns and spiritual songs, singing with grace in your hearts to the Lord. (Colossians 3:16)

When the word of God dwells in you richly your life will be a manifestation of God's grace rather than bitterness. How you respond to the offenses will either make you bitter or it will make you better. Act rather than react.

Release The Offending Party

Be ye angry, and sin not: let not the sun go down upon your wrath. (Ephesians 4:26) Forgive the offense and release the offender before you go to bed. Do not end the day with your anger eating at you. Release your offender. If you do not release the offender there has been no real forgiveness. David said it this way, **Cease from anger, and forsake wrath: fret not thyself in any wise to do evil. (Psalm 37:8)** The **cease** simply means to *stop or to abstain.* Don't sit around and wait for your offender to apologize. Forgiveness is an act whereby you release your offender. Whether or not he is guilty has no bearing on the case. You set him free and turn him loose—not for his sake, but for yours.

> **The discretion of a man deferreth his anger; and it is his glory to pass over a transgression. (Proverbs 19:11)**

The word **deferreth** means *to leave to another's judgment and determination.* When someone offends me I have to realize that it is not my responsibility to settle the matter, get even, or pass judgment. Not only are we to defer our anger, but Solomon said, **and it is his glory to pass over a transgression.** To **pass over** simply means that we *overlook the transgression.* Because I am a child of God, it is His business to settle my offenses. I simply release the offender and defer the matter to God—He will take care of it.

> **Dearly beloved, avenge not yourselves, but rather give place unto wrath: for it is written, Vengeance is mine; I will repay, saith the Lord. (Romans 12:19)**

The Bible tells us that Saul, who had become a persecutor of Christians, was on his way to Damascus, enraged with hatred, to persecute the Christians there, when he came face to face with the Lord Jesus Christ. Jesus spoke to Saul and said, **Saul, Saul, why persecutest thou me?. (Acts 9:4)** Notice how Christ took Saul's actions personally. **Why persecutest thou me?** Saul wasn't just persecuting God's people, he was persecuting Christ Himself. As God's people when we are wronged, Christ is offended. Lest anger destroy us and bitterness sour our whole life we are release the offending party and allow God to handle it —He will repay.

Remember The Forgiveness Of God

And be ye kind one to another, tenderhearted, forgiving one another, even as God for Christ's sake hath forgiven you. (Ephesians 4:32) This verse not only commands us to forgive, it tells us how to forgive. Paul starts with the command **be ye kind.** The word **kind** means to be *"disposed to do good to others, and to make them happy by granting their requests, supplying their wants or assisting them in distress; having tenderness or goodness of nature; benevolent."* It carries the idea of being gentle, caring, courteous, good, and giving. It is the exact opposite of what anger makes us want to do. Being kind one to another is a command many times repeated in the word of God.

> **Be kindly affectioned one to another with brotherly love; in honour preferring one another. (Romans 12:10)**

> **Put on therefore, as the elect of God, holy and beloved, bowels of mercies,**

kindness, humbleness of mind, meekness, longsuffering. (Colossians 3:12)

Next, we are commanded to be **tenderhearted**. Webster says that the word tender speaks of *"one that attends or takes care of,"* as a nurse would a patient. Now we're not only commanded to be kind to the fellow that made us angry, we are commanded to serve him. Being **tenderhearted** means that we show compassion, mercy, sympathy, love, and tenderness, toward our offender. It means that we are aware of their difficulties and problems and we exercise mercy in our dealings with them.

> **Blessed are the merciful: for they shall obtain mercy. (Matthew 5:7)**

> **Be ye therefore merciful, as your Father also is merciful. (Luke 6:36)**

> **By this shall all men know that ye are my disciples, if ye have love one to another. (John 13:35)**

Once we are **kind** and **tenderhearted** we can be actively **forgiving one another, even as God for Christ's sake hath forgiven you.** Notice that **forgiving** is in the present tense. Forgiving others is something that we will have to do over and over.

Also, notice the Divine standard for forgiveness! **As God for Christ's sake hath forgiven you.** I don't wait until restitution is made—I forgive because I am forgiven. I do not hold out for an apology. I simply forgive. Was I wronged? Yes! So was God and He forgave me. I forgive because I am forgiven. I follow God's example.

> **Who is a God like unto thee, that pardoneth iniquity, and passeth by the transgression of the remnant of his heritage? he retaineth not his anger for ever, because he delighteth in mercy. (Micah 7:18)**

Understand that God forgiving our sin and giving us His best is the basis for us forgiving one another of their trespasses.

Rejoice In The Lord

I will greatly rejoice in the LORD, my soul shall be joyful in my God; for he hath clothed me with the garments of salvation, he hath covered me with the robe of righteousness, as a bridegroom decketh himself with ornaments, and as a bride adorneth herself with her jewels. (Isaiah 61:10) Joy comes from a right relationship with God. was not rejoicing because he had money, a nice house, the latest fashion, or good health. His rejoicing was based upon the fact that he was clothed in the **garments of salvation**—He was a saved man. Every Christian ought to be a rejoicing Christian. Joy is an inner contentment produced by God that is not dependent upon external circumstances.

Anger will ruin your joy. We looked at Jonah a little earlier, but let's look at him in this context. He certainly serves as a good example of how anger will make you miserable, even in the most joyous situations. God had used Jonah to bring a mighty revival to Nineveh—the whole city was saved and spared. What a joyous occasion! A Divine visitation of God! This was shouting ground! You would think that such a revival would be pleasing to a preacher.

**But it displeased Jonah exceedingly,
and he was very angry. (Jonah 4:1)**

Instead of rejoicing Jonah was mad and displeased. An angry man is a miserable man. Jonah flat out tells God why he is mad.

And he prayed unto the LORD, and said, I pray thee, O LORD, was not this my saying, when I was yet in my country? Therefore I fled before unto Tarshish: for I knew that thou art a gracious God, and merciful, slow to anger, and of great

kindness, and repentest thee of the evil. (Jonah 4:2)

Jonah is mad because he did not want Nineveh spared! God spared Nineveh in spite of Jonah's wishes. Now look at Jonah.

Therefore now, O LORD, take, I beseech thee, my life from me; for it is better for me to die than to live. (Jonah 4:3)

Here sits Jonah mad, miserable, and wishing he could die right in the middle of what ought to have been the greatest highlight of his life. Jonah was so prejudiced and angry toward the people of Nineveh as his enemy that he couldn't enjoy their salvation. His anger at them ruined his ability to rejoice. And it wasn't just a short term anger.

So Jonah went out of the city, and sat on the east side of the city, and there made him a booth, and sat under it in the shadow, till he might see what would become of the city. (Jonah 4:5)

Jonah had every hope that Nineveh would eventually mess up and be destroyed by God. Eaten up with anger and bitterness, Jonah sat and watched the city, just waiting for it destruction. Jonah wasted away there in his misery and we have no indication that he ever repented of his bitterness and to get with God.

The bottom line is that we have everything to rejoice about and nothing to be bitter about. Just being saved is so much more than we deserve that we should be so busy praising the Lord, that we don't have time to get angry. No human ever suffered more than the Apostle Paul and yet he never got bitter. No doubt, his ability to rejoice saved him a lot of trouble. Paul's persecutors were actually going out and preaching the gospel. They were doing it to cause more trouble for Paul.

> **Some indeed preach Christ even of envy and strife; and some also of good will: The one preach Christ of contention, not sincerely, supposing to add affliction to my bonds: But the other of love, knowing that I am set for the defence of the gospel. What then? notwithstanding, every way, whether in pretence, or in truth, Christ is preached; and I therein do rejoice, yea, and will rejoice. (Philippians 1:15-18)**

The gospel had landed him in jail and the persecutor's preaching was adding affliction to his bonds, but Paul rejoiced that Christ was being preached. David said:

> **Thou wilt show me the path of life: in thy presence is fulness of joy; at thy right hand there are pleasures for evermore. (Psalm 16:11)**

The Joy of the Lord was David's strength (Nehemiah 8:10) An angry person has not joy. Like a destructive weed, bitterness chokes the joy out of a persons life leaven it empty and miserable.

Remove Yourself From Angry Influences

Make no friendship with an angry man; and with a furious man thou shalt not go: Lest thou learn his ways, and get a snare to thy soul. (Proverbs 22:24-25) The major problem with anger is that you can't contain it. It spreads like a wildfire until it affects everyone that comes in contact with it. This is why God warns us to separate and stay away from angry people. Lets note of three main thoughts here.

A Forbidden Relationship

Make no friendship with an angry man; and with a furious man thou shalt not go... (Proverbs

22:24a) This is a clear command. This is a serious and solemn call for separation from an angry person. This is a two fold command. 1) We are not to have a relationship with him, 2) and we are not to associate with him. Total separation is the only way to protect yourself from an angry person. Separation is not so we can be self-righteous. Biblical separation is based upon one of God's essential attributes—HIS HOLINESS.

> **But as he which hath called you is holy, so be ye holy in all manner of conversation. (1 Peter 1:15)**

We have an obligation as Christians to live holy and separated lives. Separation is designed by God, not only for holiness, but also for our protection. The word separate comes from the same word as *holy* and simply means to *set apart* for God's service. If we are going to be faithful in our service to God we are going to have to get it through our head that some relationships are forbidden. Here in this verse it is clear that we are not to make friends with or run with angry people. This is simply a matter of obeying God.

A Frightening Reality

Lest thou learn his ways... Anger is contagious! Anger breeds anger! Charles Bridges said that friendship with an angry man is *like living in a house that is on fire. His unreasonable conduct stirs our own tempers. One fire kindles another.* The fire will burn until it as burned up and has destroyed everything in its path. Anger will never produce peace—it only produces more anger.

- A Parent's anger will be reproduced in his children.
- A teacher's anger will be reproduced in his or her students.
- A Pastor's anger will be reproduced in his people.

On and on we could go. This is a fact plainly stated! The reason to separate is **Lest thou learn his ways...** You are now or soon will be what your friends are. The Bible warns:

> **Be not deceived: evil communications corrupt good manners. (1 Corinthians 15:33)**

We are commanded to stay away from angry people lest we become just like them.

> **Iron sharpeneth iron; so a man sharpeneth the countenance of his friend. (Proverbs 27:17)**

When a piece iron is rubbed against another piece of iron, it shapes and sharpens it. Just like a file rubbed across a knife blade shapes and sharpens it the people you associate with will affect you. Your friendships and acquaintances will influence you, whether good or bad. **He that walketh with wise men shall be wise: but a companion of fools shall be destroyed. (Proverbs 13:20)**

A Fatal Result

Solomon warns that the next step is to **get a snare to thy soul.** The fatal result of associating with angry people is that we will end up trapped in the same sinful anger and bitterness that the others are caught up in. Solomon describes it as a **snare to thy soul.** A snare is a trap. Webster defines a snare as *Any thing by which one is entangled and brought into trouble.* Trappers use snares to capture their prey. A snare is a place of death.

And take note that it is the **soul** that is snared and destroyed. My friend, your soul is who you are. It is the part of you that makes up your personality. Your very being will end up destroyed if you allow anger to reside and rule in your life. Angry people influence others—even to the destruction of their souls. That is serious! All over the world today are people whose souls have been ensnared and trapped in an angry lifestyle because of their association with someone who is angry. Anger is a dangerous demon that destroys everything in its path.

The Freedom Of Forgiveness

Matthew 18:21-35

Therefore is the kingdom of heaven likened unto a certain king, which would take account of his servants. (Matthew 18:23) In response to Peter's question about forgiveness, our Lord gives a parable that emphasizes a great and wonderful truth. He likens God to a just king who takes account of his servants. He keeps an eye on the books and he holds his subjects accountable for their debts. However, he is unlike other Kings in that he is a very loving and compassionate, even freely forgiving huge debts. From this parable about God's forgiveness we learn several great truths that will help us forgive others.

The Reach Of Forgiveness

Then came Peter to him, and said, Lord, how oft shall my brother sin against me, and I forgive him? till seven times? Jesus saith unto him, I say not unto thee, Until seven times: but, Until seventy times seven? (Matthew 18:21-22) Peter thought that he was going the extra mile in offering to forgive an erring brother **seven times.** However, man's ways are not God's ways and our Lord took the opportunity to teach the important truth of the unlimited forgiveness of others. Peter is basically asking, *"When my brother sins against me, how many times do I have to forgive him? Will seven times be enough?"* Jesus answered, **I say not unto thee, Until seven times: but, Until seventy times seven.** Jesus is not saying that we are to forgive only 490 times, but that our forgiveness is to be unconditional and unlimited. Forgiveness is more than an act; it is an attitude. As a child of God my spirit is to be one of love and forgiveness. Like God's forgiveness, our forgiveness is to reach beyond the offences of others. Therefore, we do not deal with others according to some set of rules and laws, but with grace. It is a limitless forgiveness, just as God forgives His children.

The Reckoning Of Forgiveness

And when he had begun to reckon, one was brought unto him, which owed him ten thousand talents. But forasmuch as he had not to pay, his lord commanded him to be sold, and his wife, and children, and all that he had, and payment to be made. (Matthew 18:24-25) This should direct our thoughts back to the enormous debt we owed the day we came to Christ. The word **reckon** means *"to count; to number."* It carries the idea of adding up the debts in order to settle an account. What an awful position we would be in if God called upon us to settle our account! Our Lord uses the amount of **ten thousand talents** to express the enormity of our debt. From the Bible we learn that the total amount of gold given to build the Temple was just over 8,000 talents (1 Chronicles 29:4, 7). That is a lot of gold—millions of dollars' worth. The huge amount emphasizes the enormity of our debt to God. Like the servant in this parable we owe a debt that we cannot pay.

> **They that trust in their wealth, and boast themselves in the multitude of their riches; none of them can by any means redeem his brother, nor give to God a ransom for him. (Psalm 49:6-7)**

We are helpless to pay the price of redemption— we are a bunch of bankrupt beggars. If God were to look at the ledgers and call us in to pay up, we would be in a lot of trouble.

The Release Of Forgiveness

The servant therefore fell down, and worshipped him, saying, Lord, have patience with

me, and I will pay thee all. **Then the lord of that servant was moved with compassion, and loosed him, and forgave him the debt. (Matthew 18:26-27)** When the debt was calculated and judgment passed, the servant fell down before the King, asking for more time and promising to pay his debt. Understand that what this servant was promising was impossible. This man was a mere servant—a common man. He was in a hopeless situation. In a state of complete panic, reaching for anything he could get his hands on, he promised to pay up. In reality he could not have paid a debt this size if he had a hundred life times to save up for it, but in his heart he was set on it. His ability was faulty but his attitude was right. Then the King was **moved with compassion.** Nothing moves the heart of God like sincere brokenness and repentance.

Then the lord of that servant was moved with compassion, and loosed him, and forgave him the debt. (Matthew 18:27) We need to understand how this works. The thought here carries us back to the law. When someone offends me he becomes my debtor. According to the **eye for an eye, and a tooth for a tooth** requirements of the law, the offending party now owes me. According to the law I have a right to collect. However, the Bible teaches us that we

66

do not live by the law, but by grace. Remember what Solomon said.

> **The discretion of a man deferreth his anger; and it is his glory to pass over a transgression. (Proverbs 19:11)**

The word **deferreth** means *"to leave to another's judgment and determination."* Because we are governed by grace we do not worry about getting even or pursuing judgment. Not only are we to defer our anger, but Solomon said, **and it is his glory to pass over a transgression.** To **pass over** simply means that we *"overlook it."* I simply release the offender—he no longer owes me. Notice that the King **loosed him, and forgave him the debt. (Matthew 18:27)** The loosing and the forgiveness go together. You cannot have one without the other. If you have truly forgiven your offender, you have set him free from obligation—he no longer owes you the debt. Forgiveness means that you give up your right to get even. If you do not cancel the debt and release the offender, it is not real forgiveness, and you will end up bitter over it. Earlier we learned that *"Bitterness is anger that is so deep and so pervasive that it colors a person's entire perception of life."* If you fail to forgive and release your debtor, you will become bitter. In fact, your bitterness will infiltrate your life to the point that you will treat everyone as if they owed you the debt. That is what bitterness does! It eventually sours the whole life. Forgiveness of the debt requires the release the debtor. If you do not release the debtor you have not forgiven the debt. Without a full and free release of the debtor there has been no real forgiveness, and bitterness will develop and defeat you.

The Reason For Forgiveness

But the same servant went out, and found one of his fellowservants, which owed him an hundred pence: and he laid hands on him, and took him by the throat, saying, Pay me that thou owest. And his fellowservant fell down at his feet, and besought him, saying, Have patience with me, and I will pay thee all. And he would not: but went and cast him into prison, till he should pay the debt. (Matthew 18:28-30) This servant having just been forgiven of so much went right out and found a fellow servant who owed him a small amount and demanded payment. Keep in mind that this servant had been forgiven an enormous amount totaling into the millions of dollars. Now he is reading to make a big fuss over **an hundred pence**—about fifty dollars. But **... his fellowservant fell down at his feet, and besought him, saying, Have patience with me, and I will pay thee all.** He heard the same plea that he had just offered to the King, but this servant rejected the cry for mercy and refused to forgive.

It is amazing just how fast we forget how God has so graciously dealt with us. R.V.G. Tasker said:

> *"This cruel wretch was still basking in the sunshine of the royal mercy, when he dealt with his fellow-servant so unmercifully."*

God has set the standard and the example of forgiveness.

And be ye kind one to another, tenderhearted, forgiving one another, even as God for Christ's sake hath forgiven you. (Ephesians 4:32)

God's forgiveness should motivate our forgiveness. It is because we have been forgiven that we are to forgive others. Forgiving others is a matter of obedience to Christ. The teaching here is really very simple. It doesn't matter how much a person has sinned against us. Their sin against us does not even come close to what we have done against God. Yet, God has forgiven us. Why? Look at it again! **... Even as God for Christ's sake hath forgiven you.** Jesus Christ died for us—He bore our sins on Calvary's cross so that we could be forgiven. Therefore, God forgives us when we come to Christ. Even after salvation, God continues to forgive us. When He forgives, it is a full and free pardon. His forgiveness of us is the Divine standard for our forgiveness of others. When Jesus was teaching on prayer He said, **And forgive us our debts, as we forgive our debtors. (Matthew 6:12)** What a startling statement —forgive us as we forgive others! What if God forgave you like you forgive others! Would you be forgiven? If some folks were forgiven by God the way they forgive others they would go to Hell. There is no room for grudges—we must fully and freely forgive others!

The Reward Of Forgiveness

The reward of forgiveness is a bitter free life. This servant, because he refused to forgive as he had been forgiven, missed the joy and reward of forgiveness. As a result he was turned over to the tormentors.

Then his lord, after that he had called him, said unto him, O thou wicked servant, I forgave thee all that debt, because thou desiredst me: Shouldest not thou also have had compassion on thy fellowservant, even as I had pity on thee? And his lord was wroth, and delivered him to the tormentors, till he should pay all that was due unto him. So likewise shall my heavenly Father do also unto you, if ye from your hearts forgive not

every one his brother their trespasses. (Matthew 18:32-35) What takes place here vividly illustrates the bondage and ruin that results from an unforgiving heart. We must be careful that we do not miss this important truth. This servant, because of an unforgiving spirit was turned over to the tormentors and imprisoned for his debt. Just what debt are we talking about here? Is it the debt of **"ten thousand talents"** that the servant was forgiven of earlier? It couldn't be, because the King had clearly forgiven him of that enormous debt. The books had been cleared and the debtor released. It could not have been the earlier debt that this unforgiving servant now owed. Let's not forget that the King in this parable is symbolic of God. When God forgives He wipes the slate clean. The sin is gone and the sinner is set free of his sin debt.

> **For I will be merciful to their unrighteousness, and their sins and their iniquities will I remember no more. (Hebrews 8:12)**

God is good! When He forgives us He releases us! When we fail God He does not go back to our pre-conversion life to dig up all of the dirt He can find and then unforgive us for it. Such an act would go against the character of God.

So! what is this new debt that lands the unforgiving servant in prison? Just a few verses earlier he was forgiven and set free. Here he is now—back in debt and headed to prison. What happened? It is really very simple! By not forgiving as he had been forgiven he incurred a new debt. Let's look at it again!

And be ye kind one to another, tenderhearted, forgiving one another, even as God for Christ's sake hath forgiven you. (Ephesians 4:32)

This is not a suggestion—it is a command. Because He has forgiven us we owe it to God to forgive others. We are duty bound to forgive those who trespass against us. When we do not forgive it puts us back in debt to God. When Jesus taught the disciples to pray, He said:

And forgive us our debts, as we forgive our debtors. (Matthew 6:12)

What if God forgave you like you forgive others? Would you be forgiven? It is amazing man sinful man longs to enjoy the forgiveness of God, while all along refusing to forgive others. Notice the descriptive language that is used here!

The King **delivered him to the tormentors, till he should pay all that was due unto him. (Matthew 18:34)** Delivered to the tormentors describes thousands of people today, who because of their unforgiving spirit, have become bitter and are living in torment as the poison of bitterness continues to eat away that their souls. If you are going to overcome bitterness, you must forgive those who have wronged you. It must be a full and free forgiveness. The debt must be cancelled and the debtor set free. That is the way that the forgiveness of God works! There are no short cuts—it must be a full and free forgiveness with no strings attached.

I have been around religious circles quite a long time and I have never heard the word resent used by a victorious man. Or at least if he used the word it was not to express any feelings within his own heart.

In the course of scores of conferences and hundreds of conversations, I have many times heard people say, "I resent that." But I repeat: I have never heard the words used by a victorious man. Resentment simply cannot dwell in a loving heart. Before resentfulness can enter, love must take its flight and bitterness take over....

The worst feature about this whole thing is that it does no good to call attention to it. The bitter heart is not likely to recognize its own condition, and if the resentful man reads this he will smile smugly and think I mean someone else. In the meantime he will grow smaller and smaller trying to get bigger, and he will become more and more obscure trying to become known. As he pushes on toward his selfish goal his very prayers will be surly accusations against the Almighty and his whole relationship toward other Christians will be one of suspicion and distrust.

—A.W. Tozer

How To Handle What's Handling You

Proverbs 16:32

As we have already learned anger and bitterness produces a horde of other sins. Anger and bitterness is often expressed in temper tantrums, rage, envy, covetousness, lust, competitive spirits, intimidation, manipulations, greed, hunger for power, pride, self-centeredness, and a poor little ole me attitude, among other things.

> **He that is slow to anger is better than the mighty; and he that ruleth his spirit than he that taketh a city. (Proverbs 16:32)**

> **He that hath no rule over his own spirit is like a city that is broken down, and without walls. (Proverbs 25:28)**

Solomon uses the illustration of a city with broken down walls to warn us about the lack of self-control. When self-control is not practiced and anger rules in our heart, we are left in a defenseless state. There is no protection. Every kind of enemy is free to invade and plunder our lives—hence the accompanying sins of anger and bitterness. When the walls of self-control are broken down in your life you are welcoming sins of every sort to dwell within. Solomon tells us that the solution to such defeat is to **rule** our spirit—self-control.

The Definition Of Self-Control

These verses are talking about a person having rule over his spirit—they are speaking of self-control. Solomon describes the man who has self-control as ... **he that ruleth his spirit. (Proverbs 16:32)** Self-control is listed as temperance in Galatians 5:23, where Paul listed the fruit of the Holy Spirit. Temperance is the rule or mastery over fleshly desires and impulses—self-control. Noah Webster defines temperance as, *patience; calmness; sedateness; moderation of passion.* It carries the idea of self-control. It is the ability to endure provocation without reacting to it.

The Discipline Of Self-Control

Again, note the phrase, **he that ruleth his spirit. (Proverbs 16:32)** The word **ruleth** means *to be in charge.* Here, the man who has self-control is seen as a man in charge. He is a king upon his throne. He is the world's greatest conqueror. It requires disciple and diligence to rule. Paul spoke of the discipline of self-control in Corinthians.

> **And every man that striveth for the mastery is temperate in all things. Now they do it to obtain a corruptible crown; but we an incorruptible. I therefore so run, not as uncertainly; so fight I, not as one that beateth the air. (1 Corinthians 9:25-26)**

Like an athlete must be disciplined if he is to win the prize, we must be just as disciplined in ruling our spirit if we are going to succeed in the Christian life. Paul uses the phrase, **temperate in all things.** The great Olympic games and athletic competitions were very popular in the days of Paul. In preparing for these events, the contestants disciplined and prepared themselves in order to be in the best possible condition and do well in the competition. In training the Athletes were **temperate in all things.** They brought their bodies into subjection so that they might win the crown. They had the same desires that everyone else had, but they ruled their spirit—they were disciplined. Paul went on to say:

> **But I keep under my body, and bring it into subjection.... (1 Corinthians 9:27a)**

That is self-control! The same is true when it comes to anger and bitterness—you must take control and discipline yourself. Anything short of complete control over your anger and bitterness will result in the ruin of your life.

The Danger Of No Self-Control

He that hath no rule over his own spirit is like a city that is broken down, and without walls. (Proverbs 25:28) This is graphic language—this verse paints a vivid picture. The man who exercises self-control is compared to a great general taking a city. The man who fails to rule his spirit, the uncontrolled man, is compared to the city which is taken, whose walls are *broken down.* It is a city with no protection, and no defense—it is open to invasion by the enemy. When we fail to rule our spirit, we tear down the barriers of protection and defense, opening up our lives to the enemy's attack. Self-control is our defense against practicing the sins of the flesh. The lack of self-control leaves us open and at the mercy of our sinful nature.

History reveals that John Adams, the second president of the United States, was not a popular statesman, even with his own party. Few doubted the purity of his patriotism or the integrity of the man. Adams was a Christian man, and exhibited many good and godly traits. However, he did not always exercise self-control, especially with his words. While he was president, his party, the Federalist party, was ruined. He was succeeded by his great rival, Thomas Jefferson. The night before the inauguration of Mr. Jefferson, President Adams left Washington D.C. Upon reaching and checking into an inn a short distance from Baltimore, it is said he noticed a portrait of Washington hanging in the public room. Walking up to it and placing his finger on his lips, he exclaimed, *If I had kept my lips as close as that man, I should now be president of the United States.*

John Adams was not alone among rulers who have been shamed by their lack of self-control. Peter the Great in 1722 issued an decree that all masters who mistreated their servants should be considered insane, and guardians were to be appointed. Later, Peter himself so terribly mistreated his gardener, that he died from the effects of it. Then Peter said, *Alas, alas, I have civilized my own subjects; I have conquered other nations; yet, I have not been able to civilize and conquer myself.* The lack of self-control has allowed the enemy to infiltrated and destroyed the lives of untold thousands. Will you allow your lack of self-control to ruin your life?

The Deterrent To Self-Control

Solomon identifies man's greatest deterrent as **his own spirit. (Proverbs 25:28)** We carry our biggest and meanest enemy with us. We must ever be aware of the fact that our flesh is an enemy of God and His holiness. The Bible teaches that within every Christian are two opposite and opposing natures. These two natures constantly contend for the believer's will.

> **For the flesh lusteth against the Spirit, and the Spirit against the flesh: and these are contrary the one to the other: so that ye cannot do the things that ye would. (Galatians 5:17)**

The word **lusteth** speaks of a strong desire. Paul states that the Spirit and the flesh lust **against** each other, meaning they have opposite desires for us. The flesh wants us to succumb to sin while the Spirit wants us to live for Christ. Paul goes on to say that **these are contrary the one to the other.** The word **contrary** means to *oppose or confront.* Here is the reason for the conflict that Christians have in their life, as they struggle to put off the old and put on the new. The flesh dictates that we be one way, and the Spirit immediately steps up and opposes the sinful nature and demands that we walk in the Spirit. The same word used here for **contrary** is translated **adversaries** in Luke 13:17 and 1 Corinthians 16:9. An adversary is an enemy or a foe. The flesh and the Spirit are adversaries—they are enemies one of another. They are not going to compromise, and will never be at peace. Therefore, the battle rages as these two adversaries fight to gain ground in the Christian's life. It must be understood that the old nature is not in subjection to the law of God.

> **Because the carnal mind is enmity against God: for it is not subject to the law of God, neither indeed can be. (Romans 8:7)**

It is a nature that is an enemy of God and hates everything that is holy and decent.

> **For I know that in me (that is, in my flesh,) dwelleth no good thing: for to will is present with me; but how to perform that which is good I find not. (Romans 7:18)**

It was the old depraved nature that Jeremiah was speaking of when he said:

> **The heart is deceitful above all things, and desperately wicked: who can know it?. (Jeremiah 17:9)**

Jesus was talking about the old depraved nature when He said:

> **From within, out of the heart of men, proceed evil thoughts, adulteries, fornication, murders, thefts, covetousness, wickedness, deceit, lasciviousness, an evil eye, blasphemy, pride, foolishness: all these evil things come from within, and defile the man. (Mark 7:21-23)**

In his book, *All Of Grace,* Charles Haddon Spurgeon wrote:

> *The old nature is very strong, and they have tried to curb and tame it; but it will not be subdued, and they find themselves, though anxious to be better, if anything growing worse than before. The heart is so hard, the will is so obstinate, the passions are so furious, the thoughts are so volatile, the imagination is so ungovernable, the desires are so wild, that the man feels that he has a den of wild beasts within him, which will eat him up sooner than be ruled*

by him. We may say of our fallen nature what the Lord said to Job concerning Leviathan: Wilt thou play with him as with a bird? or wilt thou bind him for thy maidens? A man might as well hope to hold the north wind in the hollow of his hand as expect to control by his own strength those boisterous powers which dwell within his fallen nature.

The depraved nature of man is his greatest Deterrent To Self-Control. Our depravity does not want to be controlled. Paul said:

> **For I know that in me (that is, in my flesh,) dwelleth no good thing… (Romans 7:18)**

Paul understood what a serious problem the flesh could be. **For the good that I would I do not: but the evil which I would not, that I do. (Romans 7:19)** The flesh is a deadly foe! Even when our will is to do right, we lack the ability to do it. We must fight and put off the flesh. The Bible commands us to

> **…put off concerning the former conversation the old man, which is corrupt according to the deceitful lusts. (Ephesians 4:22)**

The old is what we were before we were saved, and the new is the new life we have in Christ. We as Christians, have the responsibility of putting off the old wicked desires of the flesh and putting on the new qualities of the Spirit. Happy indeed is the person who can in all sincerity say, **For I know that in me (that is, in my flesh,) dwelleth no good thing…. (Romans 7:18)** The flesh, whether in the saint or sinner, is identical—hopelessly corrupt and at enmity with God.

The Directions For Self-Control

Again, it is **he that ruleth his spirit** that has self-control. If you are going to have self-control you must take charge of your emotions. Every believer must make a decision as to which one of these natures he is are going to side with. The Bible tells us that the only method for dealing with the old nature is crucifixion. This crucifixion is two-fold.

It Is A Crucifixion That Is Providently Inflicted

Paul said, **I am crucified with Christ: nevertheless I live; yet not I, but Christ liveth in me: and the life which I now live in the flesh I live by the faith of the Son of God, who loved me, and gave himself for me. (Galatians 2:20)** This is the same event spoken of in Romans.

Knowing this, that our old man is crucified with him, that the body of sin might be destroyed, that henceforth we should not serve sin. (Romans 6:6)

In these passages, the Bible speaks of a definite act of Almighty God in every believer, when he repents and comes to Christ as his Saviour. As far as God is concerned, every believer's old nature is dead and nailed to the cross. Because of the new birth and the indwelling presence and power of the Holy Spirit, the flesh has been rendered powerless

It Is A Crucifixion That Is Personally Inflicted

Paul said, **And they that are Christ's have crucified the flesh with the affections and lusts. (Galatians 5:24)** It is important that we realize the fact that this crucifixion must be self-inflicted. This is our responsibility! We are to crucify the flesh. In the book of Romans, Paul helps us to understand our responsibility.

Likewise reckon ye also yourselves to be dead indeed unto sin, but alive unto God through Jesus Christ our Lord. (Romans 6:12)

God has declared the believer dead in Christ. Now it is our responsibility to **reckon** our own selves dead. It is not enough to be declared crucified and dead. We must by faith reckon it to be true in our own life. The word **reckon** means to *count, to number, or to calculate.* According to Noah Webster, it carries the idea of *reasoning with one's self and conclude from arguments.* It is like reconciling a checkbook. We take the bank statement and our checkbook, sit down and make the checkbook agree with the bank statement. That is what God is saying when He commands that we **reckon** ourselves to be dead. He has already declared it. The only thing left is for us to bring our life in line with His word. Reckoning is the step of faith that acknowledges that God says about me in the Bible is now true in my life. Once I have crucified the old man, anger and bitterness will no longer govern my life. When I am crucified I am dead to my desires and my depraved nature is no longer resisting the Holy Spirit. This brings us to the next point:

The Dynamic Of Self-Control

This I say then, Walk in the Spirit, and ye shall not fulfil the lust of the flesh. (Galatians 5:16) Now we are getting down to where the rubber meets the road. Here we have the clear command of God to **walk in the Spirit.** The Christian life is often spoken of as a pilgrimage as we are travel from earth to

Heaven. The word walk, in the scripture, is many times synonymous with lifestyle. A good example is when the Pharisees questioned Jesus,

Then the Pharisees and scribes asked him, Why walk not thy disciples according to the tradition of the elders, but eat bread with unwashen hands? (Mark 7:5)

The disciples lifestyle was not in keeping with the tradition of the Pharisees. So, to speak of one's walk, is to speak of his lifestyle or testimony.

There is therefore now no condemnation to them which are in Christ Jesus, who walk not after the flesh, but after the Spirit. (Romans 8:1)

So then, our lifestyle should be produced by the Holy Spirit as He controls our life. Paul's instruction to **walk in the Spirit** is a command to live under the Holy Spirit's influence and control as a continual way of life. This is the whole idea of the filling of the Spirit.

And be not drunk with wine, wherein is excess; but be filled with the Spirit. (Ephesians 5:18)

To be filled with God's Holy Spirit means that I am fully surrendered and committed to Him. It means that the Holy Spirit has control of my life.

The clear command of Scripture is to **walk in the Spirit.** Obeying that command would settle the matter of walking in the flesh vs. walking in the Spirit. We must yield ourselves to Him, allowing Him to take over and control us. It is the Spirit of God that furnishes the power to live the Christian life.

> **Not by might, nor by power, but by my spirit, saith the LORD of hosts. (Zechariah 4:6)**

The text is clear! If we do walk in the Spirit we will not **fulfil the lust of the flesh.** Among other things, this means that anger and bitterness will not control our life. Herein lies the means of victory over anger and bitterness! **WALK IN THE SPIRIT.** Anyone who desires to have self control must rely upon the Spirit of God. In actuality, self-control is Spirit-control. A Spirit filled Christian is under the influence of the Spirit. His thoughts, words and actions are the result of the Holy Spirit's leading. To be filled with the Spirit is to be controlled by Him.

While on a stagecoach journey, the famous professor, Dr. Henry Drummond, was surprised to learn that his driver had once been a prominent business man, but because of a particular sin and his lack of self-control, this man had lost his business and had been forced to seek employment as an laborer. During their conversation the driver appealed to Dr. Drummond for help. After quoting several passages of Scripture dealing with the sin this man was addicted to, Drummond asked the driver this question, *Suppose your horses ran away, you lost control of them, and they turned down a steep hill, what would you do?* The man confessed that he would probably be unable to do anything. *But, suppose,* said Drummond, *someone sat by your side who was stronger than you and had the ability to bring the runaway horses under control—what would you do?* The driver immediately replied, *I would give him the reins.* Mr. Drummond said, *My friend, there is something within you—an evil something that is running away with your life. You've lost control until your thoughts, passions, and appetites are running riot, but,* he said, *there is One, the Lord Jesus Christ, Who is able to do for you what needs to be done if you will just turn the reins of your life over to Him.*

My friend, this is the only solution to the anger and bitterness problem. We must realize that what we need we are absolutely powerless to perform. Until we realize and acknowledge this truth we are going to meet failure. The only way to handle what's handling you is for you to turn the reins of your life over to Jesus Christ, and let Him control your life through the power of the Holy Spirit. Will you hand Him the reins of your life now?

Walk in the Spirit, and ye shall not fulfil the lust of the flesh.

Galatians 5:16

Pulling Down The Strongholds

2 Corinthians 10:3-5

Thinking determines direction. The Bible clearly teaches that a man is, in practice, what he is in his heart. Solomon warned us:

> **Keep thy heart with all diligence; for out of it are the issues of life. (Proverbs 4:23)**

Why must we keep our heart? Because out of it are the issues of life. Life will be what the heart dictates.

> **For as he thinketh in his heart, so is he. (Proverbs 23:7a)**

The heart is the control center of life. Jesus said:

> **... From within, out of the heart of men, proceed evil thoughts, adulteries, fornication, murders, thefts, covetousness, wickedness, deceit, lasciviousness, an evil eye, blasphemy, pride, foolishness: All these evil things**

come from within, and defile the man. (Mark 7:21-23)

It is in the thought life that bitterness is conceived, and develops into an uncontrollable monster. It requires no thought to become angry, but bitterness requires much thought. Bitterness is the poison that is produced when one constantly remembers and stews about an offense until it eventually turns into a deep seated bitterness that permeates and sours his whole life. We are commanded to **put away. (Ephesians 4:31)** anger. If we fail to obey God we will end up bitter. Frederick Buechner, in his book, Wishful Thinking said:

> *Of the seven deadly sins, anger is possibly the most fun. To lick your wounds, to smack your lips over grievances long past, to savor to the last toothsome morsel both the pain you are given and the pain you are giving back. In many ways it is a feast fit for a king. The chief drawback is that what you are wolfing down is yourself. The skeleton at the feast is you.*

Again, bitterness is not something that someone can do to you. Only you can do it to yourself. If you are bitter, it is because you have failed to put away anger. Bitterness is anger in its most poisonous stage.

It is a deep seated anger that has stewed deep down inside until its poison now rules the heart—it is the most dangerous form of anger. Since it is in the thought life that bitterness is conceived and developed, the thought life must be reformed. The Scriptures give us several steps to change our thinking.

Realize Your Own Inability

For though we walk in the flesh, we do not war after the flesh: (For the weapons of our warfare are not carnal…. (2 Corinthians 10:3-4) When the Bible speaks of the flesh in spiritual terms it is referring to the depraved fallen nature of man. The flesh speaks of what a man is, apart from God. Paul is dogmatic here. As God's children, He says, **we do not war after the flesh.** The flesh is powerless to accomplish spiritual things. Jesus said, **the flesh profiteth nothing. (John 6:63)**

Rely Upon The Spirit

Anger is a spiritual problem and it requires a spiritual solution to deal with it. Paul tells us where to go for power over the flesh. Our weapons are not carnal, **but mighty through God. (2 Corinthians 10:4)** This is a reference to the Spirit of God. Paul said **And be not drunk with wine, wherein is excess; but be filled with the Spirit. (Ephesians 5:18)** This verse takes us from the valley of human depravity (drunkenness) to the highest point of Christian holiness (the fullness of the Spirit) Understand that God is not offering a suggestion. He is giving an authoritative command. The command is two fold:

1) It is <u>**negative,**</u> **be not drunk with wine**

2) It is <u>**positive,**</u> **be filled with the Spirit.**

Like strong drink controls the drunkard, Christians are to be controlled by the Spirit. While strong drink effects man's flesh (depravity), the Holy Spirit effects his soul. To be filled with the Holy Spirit does not mean that we have more of Him, but that He has more of us at His will. Paul compares two kinds of influence:

1) The influence of wine.

2) The influence of the Spirit.

Paul is saying just as alcohol will control your thoughts and actions, just as the drunkard gives himself over body, soul and spirit, all he is and all he has, to alcohol, so give yourself over to the Holy Spirit. A Spirit filled Christian is controlled and dominated in thought, word and deed by the Holy Spirit. To be filled with the Spirit is to be controlled by Him. The **filled** means *to be full to the top; lacking nothing; nothing short of complete.* If there is room for any other thing in our heart, then we are not filled with the Spirit. In other words, if there is anger and bitterness occupying our heart, then we are not Spirit-filled. When we are filled He is in absolute control. His will is our will. His thoughts are our thoughts. His desires are our desires. Until the child of God realizes and accepts this truth of being Spirit-filled, he will be absolutely powerless to conquer anger and bitterness. **Not by might, nor by power, but by my spirit, saith the LORD of hosts. (Zechariah 4:6)**

Recognize The Strongholds

By the Holy Spirit's power we can be, **mighty through God to the pulling down of strong holds. (2 Corinthians 10:4)** This is military language. A strong hold is a fortress, erected from which the enemy may launch an attack. What an apt description of the anger and bitterness that permeates and occupies so many lives—a strong hold! A strong hold is a place where the enemy is dug in and prepared for battle. However, notice the phrase **pulling down of strong holds.** It speaks of demolishing and destroying an enemy's fort. You need to recognize and identify the strongholds of anger in your life and pull them down. Where has the enemy dug in and set up a stronghold in your life? Get busy identifying the areas of anger and bitterness in your life. What makes you angry? Is it someone? Is it something? Once you figure out what makes you angry, you have identified the strong hold.

Restrain Your Thoughts

Casting down imaginations, and every high thing that exalteth itself against the knowledge of God, and bringing into captivity every thought to the obedience of Christ. (2 Corinthians 10:5) This is more military language. The term **casting down** speaks of a struggle to defeat. If you are going to defeat anger there must be an be all out war launched against your thought life. You must fight like a soldier, to bring your imaginations under control. Paul says, **bringing into captivity every thought to the obedience of Christ.** Instead of sitting around sulking and stewing in your anger, pitying yourself because you imagine you have been so terribly mistreated, you recognize that the enemy has set up a stronghold in your mind, you attack that strong hold and take the enemy captive. Your goal is, bringing into to captivity every thought. The idea here is that of taking an enemy soldier as prisoner, and bringing him into obedience. No longer is he a combatant, he is a prisoner. He is no longer warring against you, he is your prisoner. He no longer controls you, you control him. Rather than sitting around thinking about how bad you've been treated and how you deserve so much better, you need to recognize that your thought life is sinful, and launch an attack to take your thoughts captive.

Renew Your Mind

And be not conformed to this world: but be ye transformed by the renewing of your mind, that ye may prove what is that good, and acceptable, and perfect, will of God. (Romans 12:2) Paul says **be ye transformed by the renewing of your mind.** The Christian's mind is renewed as he takes his sinful thoughts captive and replaces these thoughts with the Word of God. This is the process whereby the Christian puts off the old and puts on the new. **If so be that ye have heard him, and have been taught by him, as the truth is in Jesus: That ye put off concerning the former conversation the old man, which is corrupt according to the deceitful lusts; And be renewed in the spirit of your mind; And that ye put on the new man, which after God is created in righteousness and true holiness. (Ephesians 4:21-24)** Paul compares the spiritual growth of a Christian to stripping off the dirty clothes of a sinful past and putting on the white robes of Christ's righteousness. Paul spoke of this process as a transformation. He said to, **be ye transformed by the renewing of your mind.**

The word **transformed** comes from the word *metamorphoo.* It carries the idea of taking on another form. The word is used to describe the change of an ugly caterpillar into a beautiful butterfly. It speaks of undergoing a radical change. This change is accomplished by the **renewing of your mind.** We must be transformed and changed inwardly. Paul is taking this matter to the heart—it is dependent upon your thought life! This is not a fleshly attempt to control your actions, but a transformation of your thought life—a renewing of your mind. It means more than a change in our manners—it is a change in our mind. This is not outward Conformity—inward Cleansing. Our actions are the fruit of our thoughts. Right thinking produces right actions. But let no one think this is going to be easy, this is all out war—the enemy must be taken captive. A. W. Tozer, in his book *The Pursuit Of God,* wrote:

> *The ancient curse will not go out painlessly; the tough old miser within us will not lie down and die in obedience to our command. He must be torn out of our heart like a plant from the soil; he must be*

extracted in agony and blood like a tooth from the jaw. He must be expelled from our soul by violence, as Christ expelled the money changers from the temple. And we shall need to steel ourselves against his piteous begging, and to recognize it as springing out of self-pity, one of the most reprehensible sins of the human heart .

Do you want to defeat the anger and bitterness that has set up a strong hold in your life? If so, you must undergo a radical change within your thought life. You need to storm the strongholds and take the enemy captive. You must bring your thought life into obedience to Christ.

Finally, brethren, whatsoever things are true, whatsoever things are honest, whatsoever things are just, whatsoever things are pure, whatsoever things are lovely, whatsoever things are of good report; if there be any virtue, and if there be any praise, think on these things. Those things, which ye have both learned, and received, and heard, and seen in me, do: and the God of peace shall be with you. (Philippians 4:8-9)

What are you thinking about?

Made in the USA
Las Vegas, NV
17 June 2022

50351591R00056